AF131434

BOOK ANALYSIS

By Luke Hilton

The Corrections
BY JONATHAN FRANZEN

JONATHAN FRANZEN

AMERICAN WRITER

- **Born in Western Springs, Illinois (USA) in 1959.**
- **Notable works:**
  - *How to Be Alone* (2002), essays
  - *Freedom* (2010), novel
  - *Purity* (2015), novel

Jonathan Franzen is an American writer best known for his 2001 novel *The Corrections*, although he was a prominent essay writer and novelist prior to this. Born in America's Midwest in the late 1950s, one can see aspects of his childhood in the way he writes about small-town America. He published his first novel in 1988 and his second in 1992 to some critical acclaim but little financial success. These first two works marked him as an author with something to say, and he was able to use this reputation in his essay writing, where he became known for his forthright and in-depth opinions on society and literature. He wrote regularly for popular literary magazines such as *The New Yorker* and *Harpers*.

His work since the turn of the millennium has become synonymous with the concept of "the great American novel" – a title to which his books aspire with their grand themes and great lengths. His novels since *The Corrections* have also adopted a sincerer and less obviously ironic style of writing and can be said to have broken with the postmodern style of his earlier novels. He regularly speaks about his philosophy on writing and the author's role within an increasingly technological society. His essay *Why Bother?* (1996) dealt with these ideas and themes, and within some circles it has become as famous as his landmark 2001 novel.

THE CORRECTIONS

A FAMILY SAGA

- **Genre:** novel
- **Reference edition:** Franzen, J. (2010) *The Corrections*. London: Fourth Estate.
- **1st edition:** 2001
- **Themes:** family, aging, illness, economics, America

When Jonathan Franzen published *The Corrections*, its success soon made him a household name. It received both the National Book Award and the James Tait Black Memorial Prize and has been a bestseller and recipient of widespread critical praise. The novel follows the Lambert family as they attempt to deal with various trials of middle-class America. The aging parents of the family are driven by their stubbornness – Enid, to have their children home for Christmas, and Alfred, not to show weakness in the face of his progressing dementia.

The children, who enjoy both extraordinary highs and devastating lows during the course of the story, live in a modern way that confuses and frightens their small-town parents. Franzen's novel deals with many of the themes of an American nation in a state of transition; a nation coming to terms with changes in economics, politics and society. The novel was published only days before the September 11th attacks, and many have praised its foresight, arguing that the novel engages with the same concerns that society after 9/11 would have to deal with.

SUMMARY

The novel opens in the Lamberts' home in St Jude, a Midwestern suburb. Enid and Alfred, now in their old age, are the only Lamberts left living there. Enid spends her days worrying about her children, attempting to live the perfect life despite her husband's worsening dementia. She regularly speaks to her children about it, trying to convince them that he is not as bad as he sounds. Her wish is that the children all spend Christmas together *one last time* before she may or may not give in to her son Gary's suggestions of putting Alfred in a care home. Alfred receives some post with a low offer for a potentially valuable patent, but despite Enid's protestations, he is determined to sell it and split the money with his previous employer.

The children grew up in the family home, with Alfred working in a senior position at Midland Pacific Railroad, where he developed the technology that is the object of his patent. At the same time, the Lambert's only daughter, Denise, worked alongside Alfred. She has embarked on an affair with an employee of the firm. The family learn that the railroad is to be purchased by a venture capitalist firm and that if Alfred is able to work there a little longer his pension will be sizably bigger. He is already close to retirement and enjoys his work, but he mysteriously quits early, and in his usual stubborn manner, refused to discuss it. Years later it is discovered that Alfred quit early because of the affair that his daughter had with the employee, but he never mentioned it.

In their retirement, Enid continuously asks more of Alfred than he is capable of, and Alfred believes himself perfectly able to do these tasks most of the time, despite the difficulty he has in simple tasks such as bathing or using the toilet. Enid pins all her hopes on a new drug that is supposedly coming to market that may help Alfred, and discusses the merits of the drug with her son Gary. She decides that she and Alfred should take a cruise, and they meet many interesting people. Alfred hallucinates while on board and struggles to properly use the toilet. Enid enjoys talking and drinking with the other passengers but worries that she does not fit in, but she discovers a drug on board called Aslan which makes her feel wonderful. While she is in a seminar, she sees Alfred fall over the side of the boat into the ocean.

THE ASPIRING WRITER

Chip Lambert is a successful professor of literature at a prestigious college chasing the dream of tenure. He falls for a student of his and they spend time illicitly making love and taking cocktails of drugs. They both know that their actions could get Chip into a lot of trouble, but Chip's recklessness prevails and the relationship continues until the student gets tired of him. She tells half-truths to the college's board and Chip loses his job. He moves out of his academic residence to an apartment in New York City and finds a girlfriend.

When he tells his parents about his job loss, he reveals he is now working for the *Warren Street Journal*, which Enid mishears as the *Wall Street Journal* – which she then mistakenly brags to her friends about. Chip is in dire financial straits and struggles to pay for his life with his girlfriend and New York apartment. He is writing a screenplay based on his experiences as a professor, but it is largely ignored or outright criticised. He then meets a Lithuanian man who convinces him to move to Eastern Europe in order to sell Lithuania on the open market by writing fake websites. Although he makes lots of money, he struggles to get home in time for Christmas due to an insurgency in the country that turns violent.

AFFAIRS IN THE KITCHEN

Denise is driven and talented. Her skill as a chef came through hard work, just as her earlier ability at Midland Pacific Railroad came from dedication. She meets a rich man who offers to finance her very own restaurant in Philadelphia, as well as taking her on a trip to the food capitals of Europe. As head chef she earns rave reviews and the restaurant is a critical and financial hit. She begins sleeping with both the financier and his wife, but her decision to keep it a secret from both of them is the start of her downward spiral.

The owner of the restaurant fires Denise when he discovers that she has been sleeping with his wife as well as with him. The wife (with whom Denise enjoyed a more romantic relationship) forgives her at first but they eventually fall out because of Denise's actions. She falls into a depression which lasts all throughout the build-up to Christmas and continues when she discovers the truth about why Alfred quit working at Midland Pacific.

PARANOIA

Gary is the eldest and most obsessively responsible of the Lambert children. He works as a banker and is very successful in his mid-sized firm. As a responsible boss and caring husband and father, he appears to have the most stable life and mind. However, he finds that he is depressed and cannot work out why that would be. His wife, Caroline, tells him that he is depressed, but this makes him paranoid and he believes that she and their children are talking about him behind his back. Gary and Caroline argue over going to St Jude for Christmas. Caroline does not like their small-town mentality and Gary wants his mother (with whom he has a loving but frustrating relationship) to spend Christmas with her grandchildren. He gets more and more paranoid until his drinking and paranoia actually do turn his family against him. Although they are actually more worried than angry with him, Caroline agrees that Gary will go on his own at Christmas, and their youngest son can go too if he wants to.

Gary continually tells Enid that they cannot live how they do. He says that their house is too dangerous, and that Alfred should be in a nursing home. Gary believes that Alfred's patent should be sold for more money and tries to help Enid in this respect. He also learns of the drug that Enid wants to use to help Alfred and, thinking that there could be more money in this, he invests in the company's stock.

THE LAST CHRISTMAS

Alfred survived the fall out of the boat and Enid is preparing for a family Christmas. Gary arrives but has not brought his son with him, much to Enid's distress. She had prepared treats for her grandson and is upset and angry that Gary did not bring him along. Although Gary tells Enid what Caroline told him – that their son was unwell – nobody really believes this. Enid thinks that Chip will arrive from Lithuania despite nobody having heard from him, and Gary keeps telling her that she is foolish to think so.

Denise spends her Christmas upset with herself for Alfred's early retirement. Both her and Gary grow very frustrated with Enid and her requests for them to help her prepare for Christmas. She is very fond of her father and regularly defends him against her mother. Chip eventually arrives from Europe and Gary is proven wrong about his brother. Over dinner Gary tells everyone how stupid he thinks they are regarding Alfred, and that their belief he can be made better by this miracle drug is a pipe dream.

The novel concludes with Alfred going into a nursing home with an official diagnosis of Alzheimer's. He hates it there, but Chip shows some responsibility and remains with his father. Eventually Alfred dies, and Chip marries his doctor and settles down. Gary still wants Enid to sell the house but does not push it too hard, and he actually has fun with her when he and his youngest come to visit again. Denise also gets her life back on track and starts working in a hip restaurant in Brooklyn. Enid, after the death of her very unwell husband and the freedom that this grants her, decides that her life has only just begun.

CHARACTER STUDY

ALFRED LAMBERT

Alfred is best described by his stubbornness. Although he could be a loving parent and husband, as evidenced by his decision to keep Denise's affair with a colleague secret, his stern temperament is what defines him as an archetypal patriarch of the family. His stubborn nature is best illustrated by his desire to stay in the past, where things are safe. It is rare that he expresses any desires other than for completing tasks in the way he always has. When Enid insults his chair, we are told that it was the worst thing she could have said, because "the chair was the only sign he'd ever given of having a personal vision of the future" (p. 11). This demonstrates what could be seen as one of the only eclectic pieces of his personality.

His professionalism sometimes borders on obsessive, which is why he was so successful at the Midland Pacific Railroad. His dedication to his work went as far as a desire to honour the deal he made with the company for half the profits of his patent. As a man of his word, the fact that the company no longer existed in any recognisable form did not matter. With all of Alfred's dedicated work and serious demeanour, the onset of his Alzheimer's is all the more tragic. The fact that he can no longer use the toilet or the bath by himself embarrasses him, partly due to the confusion, and partly due to the erosion of his once-resolute strength of character.

ENID LAMBERT

Enid is a fragile person. As the mother of three adults with their own difficulties and the wife and primary care-giver of Alfred, this might be understandable. Her life is a constant stream of disappointments which she conveniently glosses over in an attempt to convince everybody that everything is much better than it really is. She pretends that Alfred's disease is not dementia, and that Chip's academic failure is actually a positive. One suspects that inside she knows the truth, but she clings on to the delusion for fear of being seen as peculiar and strange. Her every waking minute is an attempt at creating the image of a perfect family, *correcting* the mistakes of others and glossing over those that cannot be fixed. Alfred's stubbornness flies in the face of her desire to appear conventionally normal, as seen by her embarrassment on the cruise ship at his early departure after dinner.

The crux of the narrative in *The Corrections* revolves around Enid's desire to get the family together for one last Christmas. Although she is fully aware that it is not the best thing for everybody, and that most of the characters would rather be somewhere else, she pushes and pushes. For her it is not about having the perfect family, but having the perfect image of a family. Treated as stupid by her eldest son and an annoyance by her daughter, she perseveres in order to have the "perfect Christmas" knowing that it is more likely to go wrong than right. One could read this as a reaction to the trauma of having had so many aspects of her life controlled, and her desire to do new things is more related to the fact that Alfred never wanted to, than it is to her desire for a perfect image. For Enid the novel ends on a positive as the reader learns that she is "going to make some changes in her life"

(p. 653) once she is free of the pressures of Alfred. Perhaps she will be more fulfilled now that the image of her family has crumbled completely.

GARY LAMBERT

Alfred and Enid's eldest child is a man of contradictions. In one respect he criticises Enid constantly despite having a deep and lasting affection for her. His criticisms stem from his desire to see her have a better life, free of Alfred and the troubles that he has brought with his illness. He wants his mother to get the best so he tries to control her and cajole her into taking action that he deems the right course. His biggest dilemma comes from wanting to please his mother by having his family come to her house for Christmas, and wanting to please his wife and be a good husband and father. His wife Caroline and the older children do not want to go, and this only makes him sink deeper and deeper into his paranoid depression. His desire to help Enid blinds him to the similarities between them. Both characters experience very low points, and Gary, just like Enid, tries to hide it and pretend that nothing is wrong. He mistakes Caroline's concern for his depression as an attack. He seems to wonder how he can be so objectively successful and still be depressed.

His job is another area in which we see Gary as a man of contradictions. Working at a bank and attempting to make shrewd investments has taught him certain tricks. While trying to get Enid the best deal for Alfred's patent money he observes that the company has only offered Alfred a "tiny percentage of the patent's actual value" (p. 172) and refers to them as "shysters" (*ibid.*). Despite knowing the damage that these shady tactics are doing to his family, he admits that "in [their] position, he would have done the same" (*ibid.*). Gary is a man who often does the wrong thing for the right reason, and the right thing for the wrong reason, and like Enid, he hides behind a shield of a man who has it all together.

DENISE LAMBERT

Denise Lambert struggles throughout *The Corrections* with knowing exactly who she is. This is best exemplified in her love affair with Robin Passafaro, which is passionate and real, and yet is thrown away when she also sleeps with Robin's husband Brian. Her inability to know her desires is noticed by other people. When she becomes infatuated prior to meeting Robin and Brian with a woman named Becky, Becky tells Denise "you are *obviously* a dyke. You *obviously* always were" (p. 441). She seems to believe that she knows Denise better than Denise knows herself. Denise replies by suggesting that she is not anything, that she is "just me" (*ibid.*).

Despite Denise's inability to know her desires and her identity, she works hard and is often rewarded. At the Midland Pacific Railroad where she worked as a younger woman, she was regarded by the men who worked there as diligent and hard-working, even if this did put them to shame. She is not always liked, but she is always dedicated. One might read this obsessive dedication, which eventually shines through in her ability as a chef, as a crutch on which to balance her perceived lack of a defined personality. The fact that she does not know who she is means that she becomes obsessively involved with her work to the point of virtuosity. Of course, the underlying tension between how she presents herself and who she really is causes her to continuously spiral out of control and destroy the things she works hard for.

CHIP LAMBERT

Chip Lambert loves to see himself a certain way. Unlike his sister, his spiralling problems arise from having too *clear* a sense of who he is. His identity is carefully structured so that all those around him think exactly what he wants them to think. When teaching at the college he feels powerful and intellectual, that students hang on every word he says. Eventually, when one of those students challenges him in front of the class, he loses his identity for a brief moment. His world seems to tumble down around him and it eventually leads to him pursuing a relationship with the student that gets him fired. He saw in her the intellectual confidence that he projects, but does not actually have. He is quick to try drugs and alcohol and moves to Lithuania at the drop of a hat because he secretly is not sure who he is, but these activities, regardless of their outcome, project the image of a man who is intellectual but never boring.

After the failure of his academic career he struggles for money, but like nearly all of his family, he lives off credit in order to maintain his image. He becomes obsessive over his screenplay, which can be seen as an act of revenge for the girl who he blames for getting him fired. However, the screenplay is unbelievably pretentious because Chip "added a long theoretical opening monologue" (p. 104) in order to "salvage his artistic and intellectual ambitions" (*ibid.*). Just as he acts as though he has himself all figured out, he proceeds to make his screenplay unreadable through pretentiousness, and acts as if he is already an established screenwriter. The reader knows that, despite his cockiness and pretension, Chip is actually a pitiful and awkward character who hides from his parents because he is afraid that his carefully crafted identity will be revealed as a façade.

ANALYSIS

A DYSFUNCTIONAL FAMILY

The Lamberts are a disorganised family by any-body's reckoning, with parents who each have anxieties and troubles of their own, and children who are as neurotic as the parents. Throughout the novel Franzen presents us with a family who are either trying to control or avoid one another. They argue, they talk about each other in secret, they worry over the new members of the family getting on with the old, and they do not do ro-mantic relationships all that well. Each member of the family revolves around the patriarch, Alfred, in some way or another. Enid berates him and simultaneously wishes he would get well; Gary finds his stubbornness a frustration that is almost too hard to bear; Denise looks at him fon-dly, as somebody who stands up for her; Chip is scared of him despite Alfred's fondness for Chip. The characters all struggle with internal issues that reflect outwards onto their relationship with their family. Their need to control or escape their family mirrors their actions in their careers and love lives. They define themselves by being Lamberts.

Franzen may be suggesting something about the nature of the American family, about the way the model of the traditional family does not necessarily represent the best way of living. The Lamberts are obsessed with appearance: they live a comfortable middle-class life, the parents are faithful to each other, and they have two boys and a girl. As they grow, they each take this initial perfect family appearance and attempt to make it into what they deem to be the perfect family. Alfred's stubbornness, however, holds them back. Alfred is a representation of the America of the 20th century. His work and the ethics by which he lived his life are firmly in the past and he refuses to adjust. Each of the other characters (even Enid), however, is looking for something new; a new way of living and being. The fact that it is not until the inevitable but sad ending of Alfred's life that the other characters can find a sense of peace or purpose suggests that *The Corrections* implies that the traditions of the past may be holding back the happiness of the future.

SHADY BUSINESS

Economic issues are present throughout *The Corrections*, from Chip's money trouble to Alfred's patent. As with the family, they represent two stages of the development of American financial capitalism, and it seems as though Franzen is critical of the new models more than the hard work associated with the types of job that Alfred would have done. Chip, who lives on credit in New York City, is trying to steal a salmon fillet so that his parents will not realise he is poor when they visit. He runs into an associate who tells him about some business he has on: "We're still trying our very hardest to persuade the average American to happily engineer his own financial ruin" (p. 111). The candid way that he speaks about the seedy desires of finance in the U.S.A. suggests that foul play has become the norm in that sector. He later tells Chip "'*The implications are disturbing, but there's no stopping this powerful new technology.*' That could be the motto for our age, don't you think?" (p. 112). The forcefulness and power of the technological forms of economic development are starkly contrasted with the "honest" work done by

Alfred in the past. Franzen again seems to point to a destruction of the old in favour of the new, although here it is much more sinister.

The Corrections is contextualised by this shift in American capitalism with the boom in fortunes related to the progression of the internet. James Annesley writes on Franzen's take on the development from old to new:

> "There are internet technologies and the force of the operating system developed by the all-conquering "W _ _ _ Corporation" (not M for Microsoft on, one assumes, legal advice, but W for Windows instead). There is the transformation of post-Soviet states, particularly Lithuania, and the impact of new economy money on old economy infrastructure" (Annesley, 2006: 111)

It is very much a novel of its time in this way. Businesses found ways of maximising profit and opening the world up – the process of globalisation is at the heart of the novel. When Chip visits Eastern Europe in order to work on a website carrying out shady business, he is taking part in an economic world that would have confounded Alfred.

MENTAL HEALTH

Most of the main characters in the novel experience some kind of depression. Alfred's comes from being incapable of being the man he used to be; Enid is deeply unsatisfied; Gary is paranoid; Denise is self-destructive; Chip is broke and a failure. Each character attempts in their own way to medicate or hide from their depression, but it becomes a fundamental part of who they are.

When Gitanas, the Lithuanian, mocks Chip for having self-inflicted wounds, rather than those caused by imprisonment, Chip responds by saying "Different kind of prison" (p. 155), which makes known a serious issue in many countries today. William Davies writes: "Western economies have been afflicted by an acute problem in which they depend more and more on our psychological and emotional engagement [...] while finding it increasingly hard to sustain this." (Davies, 2015: 9). The continuous expectation to be happy makes one feel like a failure when one is sad. Davies' point implies that the new mode of living in the 21st century is one in which people must be emotionally as well as financially successful, and this becomes harder to maintain. Gary's predicament when "he'd read the dictionary definition for ANHEDONIA with a shiver of recognition" (p. 188) is that as a man with success in every other part of his life, his depression is seen as an unacceptable failure.

When Caroline shows concern for Gary, he dismisses it as mocking. However, the novel does seem to hint at the power of family to bring people together. Sam Jordison writes that Franzen

> "understands something fundamental. He knows how a father feels for his daughter, and he is able to boil it down to one beautiful, heartbreaking end-of-the-tether cry: "Just have fun and be careful." It is almost every parent's dearest wish and deepest longing for their child: Please don't get hurt. Please be happy." (Jordison, 2015)

It is love that ultimately saves Denise from her depression, and Chip too finds peace when he dedicates time to his father. Although the change from the old to the new is hard to take emotionally for society, as well as for the Lamberts, *The Corrections* seems to posit that the answer to many troubles may be within our own families.

FURTHER REFLECTION

SOME QUESTIONS TO THINK ABOUT...

- Do you think *The Corrections* qualifies as a "great American novel" and if so, why?
- Who do you find the most sympathetic character in the novel? Why?
- Why do you think Franzen chose to set the novel in places like St Jude and New York City?
- What do you think of Franzen's depiction of Lithuania?
- What is the significance of the "Corrections" in the novel's title?
- How does the work Alfred did compare with the careers of his children?
- Discuss the relationship between each of the children and both of the parents.
- Do you think *The Corrections* is successful in capturing the complexities of family life? Explain your answer.

We want to hear from you!
Leave a comment on your online library
and share your favourite books on social media!

FURTHER READING

REFERENCE EDITION

- Franzen, J. (2010) *The Corrections*. London: Fourth Estate.

REFERENCE STUDIES

- Annesley, J. (2006) Market Corrections: Jonathan Franzen and the 'Novel of Globalization'. *Journal of Modern Literature*. 29(2), pp. 111-128.

- Davies, W. (2015) *The Happiness Industry*. London: Verso.

- Jordison, S. (2015) Families in Literature: The Lamberts in The Corrections by Jonathan Franzen. *The Guardian*. [Online]. [Accessed 18 January 2019]. Available from: <https://www.theguardian.com/books/booksblog/2015/jan/01/families-in-lite-rature-the-lamberts-in-the-corrections-by-jona-than-franzen>

www.brightsummaries.com

Ebook EAN: 9782808017282

Paperback EAN: 9782808017299

Legal Deposit: D/2019/12603/31

Cover: © Primento

Digital conception by Primento, the digital partner of
publishers.